PLAGIARIST

by
Pamela L. Laskin

DOS MADRES

2012

DOS MADRES PRESS INC.
P.O.Box 294, Loveland, Ohio 45140
www.dosmadres.com   editor@dosmadres.com

Dos Madres is dedicated to the belief that the small press is essential to the vitality of contemporary literature as a carrier of the new voice, as well as the older, sometimes forgotten voices of the past. And in an ever more virtual world, to the creation of fine books pleasing to the eye and hand.

Dos Madres is named in honor of Vera Murphy and Libbie Hughes, the "Dos Madres" whose contributions have made this press possible.

Dos Madres Press, Inc. is an Ohio Not For Profit Corporation and a 501 (c) (3) qualified public charity. Contributions are tax deductible.

Executive Editor: Robert J. Murphy

Illustration & Book Design: Elizabeth H. Murphy
www.illusionstudios.net

Typset in Adobe Garamond Pro & Calibri

ISBN 978-1-933675-73-2
Library of Congress Control Number: 2012932927

First Edition

Acknowledgment is made to the following publications in which these poems appeared or will soon be appearing:

One Bright Candle......*Brownstone Poets, Spring, 2011*

In Prayer......*Jewish Currents, 2011*

Absence of Meat and Meal, Clotheslines, Historical Texts, and The Dancing Shoes......*Parting Gifts*

Metaphor......*Steam Ticket*

Homeless......*Trajectory, 2011*

Unearthing......*The Taylor Trust*

An Oedipal Moment......*www.bestpoem.com, 2009*

Zen......*www.ficklemuses.com, 2011*

Pollination......*www.bestpoem.com, 2011*

Elixirs......*Evening Street Review*

The 5K Challenge......*Poetry in Performance 39*

Birthing Exorcises......*Pinyon Review, Spring, 2012*

To Craig, Amanda, Samantha, mine for keeps!

TABLE OF CONTENTS

I. BORROWED

II. RETURNED

I

BORROWED

In my grandfather's pharmacy, I listened to stories streaming out of parched mouths, as if the mouths could not contain the words. Often they were told in other languages, but in between the Russian, the Hungarian, the Yiddish were English words that spoke the despair of leaving homelands they had loved. These were tales of great sorrow: arranged and loveless marriages; women who had babies who died in childbirth; thankless children; jobless husbands; affairs of the heart. There were euphemisms; deceptions; gracefulness; refinements all bombarding my childish ears. There was also the spirited evocation of births; beautiful babies; or intellect; unbridled passion.

From *ELIXIRS*, Pamela L. Laskin

Plagiarist

Consonants click in my consciousness
like castanets,
these are mine, but I don't want them;

what I want
is the slow, steady sound
of a horses' heart-beat
luscious land
I've never traveled to,

rural Ohio, perhaps
where calves are birthed beautifully
behind the barn.

I want to be
on the farm,
allow the boys
to burst through my body
and bleed me dry.

I will journey there
even if there is no plane;
I will sail with the wind of your words
and claim them
as my own.

Readings

On loan
this book -
my body;
I read it
knowing
the hidden cavities
of meaning
measured
in the circumference
of my toes.

I walk
with words
that lift me
off the concrete steps
of Grand Army Plaza
into my heated heart.

My heart memorizes
how many times
Atticus hugs Gem,
Gatsby eyes Daisy
Whitman echoes songs that sing
their own beautiful exaltations.

I am not just the book.
I am Brooklyn Central
baring my breasts
for the world to read.

Audience

Glenn Ligon
not tragically colored,
"lost his voice,
found his voice"
when he walked
into a canvas,
so I will race into his.

Don't run away from me, Glenn.
Come into my eyes
so I can feel your voice
in my body
like paint.

Your colors
now belong to me.

Just Pretend

Maira Kalman Exhibit, Jewish Museum, 2011

I forgot about
hammering out tunes
to make bears dance
when we long to move the stars;

what I recall
in the emptiest of metaphors
is Flaubert wrote these words
in MADAME BOVARY,

big, bold words
that I would love to borrow,

if only for a moment,
so I could feel the mountains move,

majestic mountains
whose peaks probe the stars,

not my words.

Birthing Exorcises

I should have aborted
a long time ago,
before its hungry mouth
sucked the life out of me,
before it cried out for attention,
wailing incessantly-day and night;
before there was more than one
with its own particular glazed expression;
it would have been easy
when I was twenty
to discard the dreams
like dishwater down the drain
and never look back,

before this
bundle of words
became a poem.

Silver Roses

To Rachel Wetzsteon

She was only
forty years younger
than the other self-
the shadow
that crept out of the casket,

and yearned
to own a life
of luxury
because the earth is Olympic
the sky is so large
it can't be measured;

the one
who stayed behind
could not figure out
why April showers
linger into May,
why May was never as warm
as promised,
why love could leave
as quickly as a season
if not before.

She had no patience
for winter to defrost
because winter was her wardrobe
even in summer.

In Mourning

Waterless fountain
how does it feel
to be abandoned in the field
bereft of water,
stoic beneath the umbrage
of leafless trees?

Like me,
do you mourn those days
when you spouted oceans
of wild dreams,
when every day
was a new surge
of liquid poetry?

Different Forms

My daughter writes me
so obscurely
I can't find the words
in the dictionary,

my poems
use diction
too simple for her taste;

I am readable
in a way
she is not.

Her verse
skips off the page,

and when I race
to catch it,

my hands
have grown too small
for this desire.

Unearthing

To Samantha, 18

Bring back the girl
who lifts her dress
like it's an ocean,
while the water whirls
her into rapids
of enthusiasm.

I know she's there
if I shovel deep
into knee-high snow,
and travel through twisters
of tortured sorrow.

I know she's there
waiting for you
to dig up
her smile.

An Oedipal Moment

Daughter,
you burst into beauty
the moment of conception,

proud Mama was I
as you grew,
so did the blonde locks
that cascaded down your back
like Rapunzel's
(I would never cut them)
and you were smart as Socrates.

Now
I gaze
at the reams of words-
pollen
on white orchards.

When did the garden grow
to dazzle such spectators?

Each word
translucent
with petals of perfection
while inside
a stamen of saturation
dense with the duty of meaning.

Where was this garden birthed?

Surely not in my womb,
my words now wither
like dried leaves
in winter.

Homeless

To mother

I climbed down the ladder
of your breasts,
careful not to crush them
aware
they were milkless,
but had never fed me anyway.
Aware
I was one step away
from the bottom rung
of your big belly–
hard to imagine
was once my home.

Seasonal Shifts

In memory, Susan Bright

I borrowed your words
when mine were wet and wild;
shivering, you lent me a shawl
to wrap around bones
that rattled restlessly.

Covered in your caravan
I was safe from the elements of scorn
since this shawl
was stitched by many voices;

the warmth of voices
draped in your large laughter
seeped into words
from all over the world.

When summer came
I crept out of the cape
became a body
bound by your cover.

Absence of Meat and Meal

I am prepared
to teach
what's not on the map
that spits out mountains
divided
into latitudes and longitudes,
but one
that travels
to subduction zones in the heart
where excavations
are not possible,
a dried-up river
crying out for rain
as sun bakes in sorrow.

A Teacher's Lament

What if someone
is dumb, but nice
works hard
as an underground miner
not capable of digging
but willing to try anyway
unearthing nothing?

Do you give him something
for the reward
of trying?
Perhaps a small trophy
that says,
I see your eyes
and they are hopeful
as morning,

or do you say
forget it,
why bother digging out
the script from a novel
when you can hardly read,

get lost
you keep hitting
the same brick wall
that had told you
"no trespassing"
to begin with.

M.I.A.

To Walt Whitman

I feign celebration
since I am voiceless,
so I ask to borrow
your song.

I apologize
I am not a plagiarist,
but a poor poet
bereft of words,
seeking cover
inside a poem.

You said,
"every atom belonging to me
as well belongs to you."

So it's not a crime
to lift your language
when mine is missing.

Peanut Butter and Jelly

AIDS AWARENESS WEEK

This is the face
of one child's sorrow-
eyes lounge in a hammock
suspended from skull to skull
breath to breath.

The body slips into sickness
like a thief-
the woman whose lover
loved the illness inside her,
the drug addict,
the transfused blood
nobody bothered to bathe,

and the boy
who may see tomorrow
but may not
dream the future
his friends do;

his fantasy:
a week with no absences
peanut butter and jelly
for dinner every night.

Zen

You step
into the Zen palace
like a princess
in snakeskin slippers
and leave them on the rug,
as is the practice,
but now
no one wants them
not even the stepsisters
who would prefer glass.

Yes,
even the stepsisters know
you, shoeless,
as someone
with the trellises of a princess,
the shoes, the sari,
the smile of a genie
who dismantles dreams
with a poisoned pen.

II
RETURNED

It was the magic of language that grandpa brought to his domain. People flocked to the pharmacy to be healed, and it wasn't the vials of liquid or containers of pills that soothed them. It was the vineyard of his voice, the "holy of holies", the peaceful sounds from the river deep inside. He had open ears for everyone's language, and they always left the pharmacy feeling better. And he unburdened his heart, too, sharing the gift of grace.

I was among those held captive by his tales, and I became the scribe for all his stories, since they became mine.

From *ELIXIRS*, Pamela L. Laskin

The Dancing Shoes

I can't stop
dancing,
my damaged feet
have diarrhea
of movement,
to stop now would mean
to step downstream
into angry currents
(though the water I wade in is diseased, I know),
it is my mutilated music
murky milk
whirling dervish
leaping dangerously
off the page.

The Muse

The chuppah of your words covers my heart
when I decide to wed to poetry,
the language vows I take, some may call art
it's you-my prayer, my muse, that marries me.

I read you in my memory, my mind
where every lovely vowel resonates
so I say "yes" eternal for your kind
this flight of fancy, nothing short of fate.

So strangle me in form, and straddle, too,
and break the glass with screams and shouts of glee,
the celebration's festive when with you,
ketubah seals your poetry in me.

With you, my love, forever I will wed.
You dazzle dreams and saturate my head.

The Laundress

I'm a poet
different from others,
I do lots of laundry
spend hundreds
on Heavenly clean detergent.
More than most poets,
I scrub and scour
persist
with grease and grime,
refuse to believe
in permanent stains.

I even wash
other people's
filthy laundry,
and enjoy
the caked vomit
of young children,
the smelly semen
of lovers,
the sour sweat
of a night of sex and boozing;

I am willing to wash
all of this,
and if the bleach of my broiling labors
is insufficient,
laundress that I am,
I'll get my hands wet
let the dirt destroy
these very puny nails,
again
again
again.

Clotheslines

Why wash your poem
in THE NEW YORKER
as if it's the only space for laundry?

I had pined
to place
my sheets there, too,
but now,
forty years
of ill-fitting clothes
had convinced me,

there are other places
where saturated socks
could swim across clotheslines
without a need
to dry quickly
or be noticed
for their startling colors.

Now
my bedding
flies
in the arms of the wind,
lingers like a lullaby

sings
all day
all night.

So Much Depends Upon
(with homage to William Carlos Williams)

So much
depends upon

a poor poem pandering
to find its voice

until it is wind and breath
beating in my body.

The Pulitzer

Jie has passed
he wrote
a passing essay.

This may not mean a lot
to you poets;
I know, I write poems
and never expect
words to languish.
I want them to soar
off the page
get lost in the clouds
and when they land
find a home
in someone's magazines.

But for now
for today
the fact that Jie discovered
words could make sentences
sentences could make paragraphs
paragraphs could find their way
into a community,

is better than a poem,
better than a book.

It's the Pulitzer
that Jie
has passed.

The Grand Tetons

In memory of my father, Carl Laskin

Forty years
after your heart
fell into the crater,
I am bathed
in sunshine
and snow-capped mountains,
oblivious to caves, graves,
tombstones;
until I return home
to heated sidewalks
tugging at broken-bodies:
summer sickness.

Not that I ever forget you, daddy,
but in Yellowstone and the Tetons,
climbing the mountains,
I fail to recall the day
I was a valley
who lost
my sky,
my sea.

A Tale

To my Mom, Sylvia

Once
there was a young girl
who dallied in gardens
and wrote poetry;
she believed
in rainbows and fairy tales.

Once she was a Queen
who married a King.
She begged for rescue,
but this tale did not end
happily ever after,

except
they had a princess-
the princess of poetry
who raced out of the kingdom
on a black horse,

abandoning the Queen
whose mind
was dust in the dungeon.

When the girl returned
she remembered the Queen's
quest for magic,
that once she rhymed
that this verse
never would have happened
without her,

so she took her from the tower,
and brought her
to her flowers.

In Prayer

In memory, Enid Dame

I had forgotten
how the Red Sea parted
and bowed
before it took leave,

how Lilith's picnics
erected monuments
out of latkes,
and the wicker basket
of words,

how hunger subsided
as your voice
cradled ears
like the good Mameleh
of poetry,

or the goddesses
of Brighton Beach
whose waves bowed down
their humble heads
in prayer.

Spring
To Ira

Watching you dress
undresses me,
so I will strip
silently
beneath the slip of water,

and I will ask you
to disrobe,
layer upon layer
of ludicrous attire,
until you are the earth
you are the lake

and I am spring
teasing your nakedness
daring you to dance
imploring you
to swim inside.

Lending Library
To Ira

I am never
returning this book,
I understand its passages
so well-
the swiftly swollen sentences
the pauses and exclamations
the way the paragraphs
bleed into one another,

but mostly
the text
freed from the bondage of character and form,
it takes risks
never encountered
on the written page;

and the pages
fold beautifully
inside my pocket.

The 5K Challenge
To Craig, 26

You finished
not in the lead,
but with good timing,

and I was not surprised
since the moment
you sprinted out of my stomach
twenty-six years ago,
your body was a bulldozer
breaking through my borders,

breathtakingly racing
into foreign lands
I lovingly admire.

Historical Texts

To Samantha, 21

Hidden
in the creased pages
of the womb-
a text
of undiscovered history
ready to unravel
in the world.

How could I have known
as this geyser erupted
that time would splinter
into satisfaction and unease:

a Black president,
a nation divided,
the collapse of the world trade center
wars growing into bigger wars,

you growing into a woman
writing yourself-
a beautiful, brilliant book
for this epoch.

Pollination

To Samantha Rose, 21

I dig
for words
in dungeons of darkness-
murky oceans
where sentences swim
among barnacles
algae sponges and anemones;
sometimes the water stinks
like sewers
from which I scrape the rust of my mother
away.

Your seeds
grow abundantly
fermented in rich soils
begonias bloom,
pollinated in faraway landscapes:
Namibian nuances
Jerusalem juices
Irises from Istanbul,

abundance of flowers
secret gardens
rare fragrances
reading you
writing me.

Metaphor

To Samantha, 16

I asked the poet-
the sage,
who has published more volumes
than I,
but also
has a schizophrenic mother
and writes about her
constantly,
does this-
the writing
settle the demons?
And she said, "No,"
they slither
like snakes in her sleep-
the words, the mother
swallow her
whole.

While I have found
in the folds of my flesh
a secret.

Sixteen years ago,
I birthed
a child
on the blank page
of my life,

and no metaphor
has ever measured
meaning
made my mentally-ill mother
so obsolete
as this-

my daughter
the poem that has left my language
to grow its own rhythm
its own rhyme,
to invent a form
that has freed me of bad mother,
since I have written this poem
so perfect in the way
she's a new verse
every day,

and I am the good mother
who created
her voice
her spirited simile.

Lessons from the Forest

To Samantha, 21

You can still
hike through forests.

You can still
shop at thrift stores,

bicycle around the park
pedaling past the wind,

you can make
your arms light sabers
to touch the sky
to touch the sea,

you can see
your way to the ball
wearing anything you want;
forget those glittered gowns
the crescent crown;

aren't you glad
even if you're home
after midnight,

you'll still wear
the same clothes
on your back?

I'd gladly meet you mid-way in the woods
for tea
and gingerbread cookies.

One Bright Candle

To Addie

This is the house
your mother never gave you:
twenty-five bright begonias
blooming bright colors,
music to welcome you,
the lightness of air,
painted figures
lining the mantle,
art bleeding from the walls,
arms to cradle
fruit and flowers;

a daughter
to dance with
one bright candle
swaying and singing
with the moon
as it has
for twenty-two years,

on the cake
your mother never gave you
that you bake
in the oven
of your heart.

A New Manuscript

To Samantha, College Graduation

Leaving
your luggage packed
with language
not borrowed
from Widener library
or the ivy-trellised buildings,
not the texts of Virgil, Homer, Shakespeare,
or the Celtic crosses
encrypted in vaults
adorned with dust.

You have traveled
as far as Odysseus,
though you never left
Adams House;

now you're packing
years of papers
diction
to dress, undress, redress
journey far away
from where the Bard rages.

For Keeps

I'm keeping
the husband
of thirty plus years,
the children
in their twenties-
one girl, one boy,
not newsworthy material,
but readable and friendly.

I'm keeping
the job,
my students awaken ancient
hieroglyphics
I thought I had lost
in my dictionary;

I'm discarding
the thesaurus
and keeping only the vocabulary
whose words I need not look up.

All
as good as my urban skin-
moleskin
weathered
by almost sixty years,

and though
these pages may be ripped and frayed

I've memorized them
by heart.

About the Author

Pamela L. Laskin is a lecturer in the English Department at The City College of New York, where she directs the Poetry Outreach Center. Ms. Laskin started out as a poet; consequently, hundreds of her poems have been published as well as four poetry chapbooks. GRAND CENTRAL STATION, a full-length collection, was published in 2003, and since that time REMEMBERING FIREFLIES (Plain View Press); SECRETS OF SHEETS (Plain View Press); GHOSTS, GOBLINS, GODS AND GEODES (World Audience); VAN GOGH'S EAR; (Cervena Barva Press) and DARING DAUGHTERS/DEFIANT DREAMS (A Gathering of Tribes) have been published. Publish America recently published a book of children's poetry that she co-authored with Ms. Jeanette Adams, a well-known African American children's poet, and also Ms. Elise Buchman, ANIMALS CRACKERS AND THEIR FRIENDS. Tudor Press published GETTING TO KNOW YOU, a YA novel, in 2003, and Diversion Press published VISITATION RITES, an expansion of a young adult story originally published in SASSY magazine. Her published children's books include A WISH UPON A STAR (Magination Press); HISTORICAL HEROIC HORSES (McGraw-Hill); MUSIC FROM THE HEART (Bantam) and THE BURIED TREASURE (McGraw-Hill). Dozens of her short stories have been published, too, including two YA stories, one in YOUNG MISS and the other in SASSY. She edited two collections: THE HEROIC YOUNG WOMAN (2006), a collection of original feminist fairy tales, and LIFE ON THE MOON: MY BEST FRIEND'S SECRETS (Linus Publication), a collection of young adult fiction.

Academic interests (aside from children's literature and writing and poetry), include fairy tales (a sub-genre of children's literature) and creative fiction and non-fiction.

Books by Dos Madres Press

Jennifer Arin - *Ways We Hold* (2012)

Michael Autrey - *From The Genre Of Silence* (2008)

Paul Bray - *Things Past and Things to Come* (2006), *Terrible Woods* (2008)

Jon Curley - *New Shadows* (2009), *Angles of Incidents* (2012)

Richard Darabaner - *Plaint* (2012)

Deborah Diemont - *Wanderer* (2009), *Diverting Angels* (2012)

Joseph Donahue - *The Copper Scroll* (2007)

Annie Finch - *Home Birth* (2004)

Norman Finkelstein - *An Assembly* (2004), *Scribe* (2009)

Gerry Grubbs - *Still Life* (2005), *Girls in Bright Dresses Dancing* (2010)

Richard Hague - *Burst, Poems Quickly* (2004)

Pauletta Hansel - *First Person* (2007), *What I Did There* (2011)

Michael Heller - *A Look at the Door with the Hinges Off* (2006),
    Earth and Cave (2006)

Michael Henson - *The Tao of Longing & The Body Geographic* (2010)

R. Nemo Hill - *When Men Bow Down* (2012)

W. Nick Hill - *And We'd Understand Crows Laughing* (2012)

Eric Hoffman - *Life At Braintree* (2008), *The American Eye* (2011)

James Hogan - *Rue St. Jacques* (2005)

Keith Holyoak - *My Minotaur* (2010), *Foreigner* (2012)

David M. Katz - *Claims of Home* (2011)

Burt Kimmelman - *There Are Words* (2007), *The Way We Live* (2011)

Richard Luftig - *Off The Map* (2006)

Austin MacRae - *The Organ Builder* (2012)

J. Morris - *The Musician, Approaching Sleep* (2006)

Rick Mullin - *Soutine* (2012)

Robert Murphy - *Not For You Alone* (2004), *Life in the Ordovician* (2007)

Pam O'Brien - *The Answer To Each Is The Same* (2012)

Peter O'Leary - *A Mystical Theology of the Limbic Fissure* (2005)

Bea Opengart - *In The Land* (2011)

David A. Petreman - *Candlelight in Quintero - bilingual edition* (2011)

Paul Pines - *Reflections in a Smoking Mirror* (2011)

David Schloss - *Behind the Eyes* (2005)

William Schickel - *What A Woman* (2007)

Lianne Spidel & Anne Loveland - *Pairings* (2012)

Murray Shugars - *Songs My Mother Never Taught Me* (2011)

Nathan Swartzendruber - *Opaque Projectionist* (2009)

Jean Syed - *Sonnets* (2009)

Madeline Tiger - *The Atheist's Prayer* (2010), *From the Viewing Stand* (2011)

James Tolan - *Red Walls* (2011)

Henry Weinfield - *The Tears of the Muses* (2005),
    Without Mythologies (2008), *A Wandering Aramaean* (2012)

Donald Wellman - *A North Atlantic Wall* (2010)

Martin Willetts Jr. - *Secrets No One Must Talk About* (2011)

Tyrone Williams - *Futures, Elections* (2004), *Adventures of Pi* (2011)

www.dosmadres.com